THE POEM OF QUEEN ESTHER

THE POEM OF QUEEN ESTHER

by João Pinto Delgado

Translated by

David R. Slavitt

New York   Oxford

Oxford University Press

1999

Oxford University Press

Oxford   New York

Athens   Auckland   Bangkok   Bogotá   Buenos Aires   Calcutta
Cape Town   Chennai   Dar es Salaam   Delhi   Florence   Hong Kong   Istanbul
Karachi   Kuala Lumpur   Madrid   Melbourne   Mexico City   Mumbai
Nairobi   Paris   São Paulo   Singapore   Taipei   Tokyo   Toronto   Warsaw

And associated companies in
Berlin   Ibadan

Published by Oxford University Press, Inc.
198 Madison Avenue, New York, New York 10016

Oxford is a registered trademark of Oxford University Press

Library of Congress Cataloging-in-Publication Data
Delgado, João Pinto, d. 1653 or 1654.
[Poema de la reyna Ester. English]
The poem of Queen Esther / by João Pinto Delgado;
Translated by David R. Slavitt.
p.   cm.
ISBN 0-19-512374-3
1.   Esther, Queen of Persia—Poetry.
I. Slavitt, David R., 1935-   II. Title.
PQ6388.D19P6413   1999
861'.3—dc21   98-19437

Some passages of "The Poem of Queen Esther" have appeared in *Transgression,
Punishment, Responsibility, Forgiveness: Essays in Culture, Law, and the Sacred.
Graven Images*, 4 Ed. Andrew D. Weiner and Leonard V. Kaplan. Madison:
University of Wisconsin Law School, 1998.

1 3 5 7 9 8 6 4 2

Printed in the United States of America
on acid free paper

FOR HANNAH

INTRODUCTION

❖

D URING THE 250 YEARS before the expulsion of the Jews
from Spain on January 2, 1492, their position had been
deteriorating from what it had been during the Golden Age,
which extended from the tenth through the twelfth century
in Moslem Andalusia. Even in Christian Spain, the rulers had
been tolerant and benevolent toward Jews (Fernando III of
Castile styled himself monarch of three religions and, in the
spirit of *convivencia*, the epitaph on his tomb in the Cathedral
in Seville is written in Latin, Castillian, Arabic, and Hebrew).
But as Christian Spain grew in strength and the Moors' power
waned, that tolerance gave way to nationalism and its expres-
sion of religious exclusivity in the Inquisition.

The Marranos were the crypto-Jews of Spain and Portugal
who had been forcibly converted to Christianity. In some in-
stances, those conversions were sincere and enthusiastic—Fray

Tomas de Torquemada, the first Inquisitor, was of Jewish descent. But many *conversos* continued their adherence to Jewish practices and beliefs, even though the further practice of Judaism was regarded as a criminal offense.

Even after the expulsion of the Jews from Spain in 1492 and the forced conversion of the Jewish community of Portugal in 1497, many of these secret Jews persisted in their faith and its rituals and observances. (See David M. Gitlitz's *Secrecy and Deceit: The Religion of the Crypto-Jews*, 1996, Jewish Publication Society.)

Among the Marrano poets (see also Antonio Enriquez Gomez and Miguel de Barrios), João Pinto Delgado was the best and the most interesting. Born in the mid-1580s, he spent his early life in Vila Nova de Partimão with a least one brief period in Lisbon. Around the turn of the century, his parents moved to the Spanish Netherlands and then to France, and João returned to Lisbon to continue his education and pursue his literary career.

By 1612, his parents had relocated to Rouen and had been naturalized there. Somewhere between 1624 and 1626 he joined them there, and it was in Rouen that his collection of poems was published in 1627 by David du Petit Val: *Poema de la Reyna Ester, Lamentaciones del Propheta Jeremias, Historia de Rut, y varias Poesias*.

The poet and his father were leading members of the Marrano community in Rouen, and they were undoubtedly involved in the 1633 crisis there that followed the refusal of Diego de Cisneros, a Spanish priest, to grant a certificate of orthodoxy to Diego Olivera in support of his application for naturalization.

The Marranos were deeply concerned—and deeply divided. There was resentment on the part of the sincere conversos, the practicing Christians who had fled Spain because their family origins made it dangerous for them to remain where they continued to be objects of suspicion on the part of the Inquisition, since they considered themselves again to be endangered by those who were still secretly observant as Jews—who, in turn, no doubt considered the conversos to be turncoats and apostates, cowardly and contemptible.

This campaign of Cisneros against Judaizers produced a situation in early seventeenth-century France not unlike that of Germany sixty years ago in which the assimilated German Jews, finding themselves in jeopardy, blamed their unassimilated eastern European co-religionists for their plight almost as much as they blamed the Nazis.

The Pinto Delgados moved first to Antwerp and then to Amsterdam, where João changed his name to Mosseh. From 1636 to 1637, and again in 1640, he was one of the seven *parnasim* (governors) of the Talmud Torah Seminary in Amsterdam. He died there in December of 1653.

His poetry is Jewish and in Spanish, which makes for a curious dissonance that is also recognizable to us in this century. One thinks, for example of Paul Celan trying to reclaim the German language even as he distorts it, as if to make it his own. It could also be said that his aim was to revive through literature that fantasy Jews had been able to entertain for a century or more of a welcoming cosmopolitan culture. Spain, too, had been hospitable for a while. From the eighth century, when the Arab troops of the Caliph of Damascus arrived in Spain, to

Ferdinand and Isbella's expulsion order in 1492, the Jews had experienced a series of ups and downs but had mostly benefited from the Arabs' tolerance of the "Peoples of the Book," which included Jews and Christians as well. In the smaller Christian kingdoms of the Middle Ages, Moors and Jews had lived in their separate areas and were more or less autonomous communities, self-governing and paying taxes to the crown.

Cees Nooteboom writes in *Roads to Santiago* (1997, Harcourt Brace) about watching part of a television series on heresy in Spain:

> the program ends on a nostalgic note: not only do the Sephardim miss Spain, but also Spain is homesick for the Jews. I recognize the opening images straightaway, for they show the delicate tracery on the walls of the synagogue in Toledo, *la Sinagoga del Tránsito*, of Transition. Or is it of Exodus, for that is what the programme is about. The notes I make in the dimly lit hotel lobby prove to be indecipherable when later I try to read them, but what I remember most clearly is the *claim* to a Jewish identity. All of a sudden everyone turns out to be Jewish: not just Cervantes but also Saint John of the Cross, and Saint Teresa of Avila, and that great and enigmatic poet of the Golden Age, Luis de Góngora, and if they were not fully Jewish themselves then surely their *linaje* was, their line of descent.

João Pinto Delgado might well have read Góngora's work in those years in Lisbon. The sense that tortured Celan of owning a culture and of being owned by it, of loving it and hating it, must have afflicted him too. Spain is a poor country, and poverty loves scapegoats. Nooteboom quotes Victor Chamorro as saying in *Extremadura, afán de miseria*, "Nowhere in Extremadura will you find a village without a history or legend linking the Jews with the death of infants, sacrilege, poisonings, corruption of the church." It was a dangerous and hateful place, but the memory of a better time—only three generations before João's birth—had not quite died. More likely than not, that memory only made the pain of the present moment worse.

So Pinto Delgado wrote in Spanish, and about the Bible—Jeremiah, Ruth, and Esther. But the *Poema de la Reyna Ester* is also an extended metaphor, for its account of suffering and injustice followed by a magnificent vengeance applies to the Jews' experience in Spain with the Inquisition almost as well as it does to its ostensible subject, their peril and deliverance in Persia under Xerxes (Ahasuerus).

João Pinto Delgado's name is not well known. I'd never heard of him when I came across Timothy Oelman's book, *Marrano Poets of the Seventeenth Century* (1982, Fairleigh Dickinson University Press / Associated University Presses) on a shelf at the Strand bookstore in New York one afternoon. Oelman makes no attempt to reproduce Pinto Delgado's rhymes in English and they seem to me crucial, in the terza rima of "In Praise of the Lord" and in the sestets of "The Poem of Queen Esther." He also offers only brief selections of that latter work. But those sections he provides were interesting enough for me to obtain a copy of the facsimile edition of the 1627 volume that the Institut Français au Portugal published in Lisbon in 1954. And with the help of Ellen Frye, a graduate student in

Spanish at the University of Pennsylvania who prepared for me a word-for-word trot, I was able to produce a complete English version of this extraordinary poem.

It is, I think, an ornament of Sepharad literature, and, indeed, of European literature of the Renaissance. Its dedication is to the "Illustrissimo Y Reverendissimo" Cardinal Richelieu, more probably because he was Louis XIII's general superintendent of navigation and commerce (the Pinto Delgado family were in the import and export business) than because the achievement of his life's efforts in politics was the formation of alliances with the Netherlands and with the German powers that increased France's power and prosperity to the detriment of Spain's.

Spain's economic and cultural decline may not be so catastrophic as Haman's, or anywhere near so severe as what it had deserved. But what had once been a vibrant cultural center turned into a backwater, rather like Vienna since World War II. Cees Nooteboom loves Spain because it is so melodramatic and un-Dutch. His *In the Dutch Mountains* (1987, L.S.U. Press) suggests that Spain is what the Netherlands needs to remedy its spiritual deficiencies. Pinto Delgado's progress from Iberia, through France, to Amsterdam is a demonstration of the converse of his proposition. There is much to be said for moderation, tolerance, and boring decency. The ideal combination seems not to exist on this earth, which is what drives writers to imagine it, as Nooteboom did in *In the Dutch Mountains* and as Pinto Delgado did 350 years ago in "The Poem of Queen Esther."

CONTENTS

En Alabanza del Señor
In Praise of the Lord

João Pinto Delgado (1585?–1653)

Señor, I pray you, who govern earth and sky
and through whose might the immense and truculent sea
is confined to its proper bounds so that land stays dry;
    you who can penetrate deepest obscurity
with a dazzling light distilled from the heart of the flame
of the brightest fire—as if snow itself could be
    ignited; lighten the gloom of my cave of shame
and lift this moral darkness in which I live.
I give thanks for the gift of life and bless your name,
    but unless I sense your love in what you give,
I must reject the worthless universe.
You are my wavering faith's preservative.
    My enemies wish me every ill, but, worse,
my own weakness assails me. Aim your bow
at my unreliable heart and conquer, coerce,
    and rule as I remember long ago
you used to do. Make me a man once more
of integrity and honesty with no
    vanity or falseness. The metaphor
is entropy, which everywhere is the fate
of matter. And also of spirits. Ah, Señor,
    they too give way and betray us to our great
shame, beguiled by the senses' blandishments.

Those hopes that arise in a dawn's immaculate
glow are dead by dusk, and our confidence
has vanished as, with baleful eyes, we stare
at ruin on every side. When we shall go hence
summoned before your throne of glory where
we shall stand speechless, our faults will be made known.
Ashamed of this world's corruption, we shall despair
unless the ichor of your Grace pour down
and your sweet breath refresh us as in spring
the gentle rains revivify a lawn.

A miracle, it is, a glorious thing
upon which we fix our eyes, for a noxious mist
will close them soon enough. The ravening
lynx may stop in its tracks, but souls persist
to the next world where a richer quarry awaits
than any the subtlest eschatologist
can ever propose. Though this life incubates
endless yearnings it cannot satisfy,
there, in glory, desire modulates
into content and repose—as the ominous sky
clears, when a storm has spent its force, to a blue
tranquillity that delights the inner eye.

The wind may be howling somewhere else, it's true,
but you who cowered at night behind your door
in fear of armed men you knew were coming for you
are safe in heaven now, tormented no more.
Think of the wretched here on earth who weep
but find neither comfort nor pity from men who ignore
their lamentable sufferings. Innocent sheep

4

in the fields fear predatory beasts that roam
the woods, but in town, tucked in our beds, we sleep
    in equal terror, knowing the danger from
those neighbors who are not our friends, for they
menace us at work, in the streets, and at home.
    Is it a comfort to think that somehow they
will suffer retribution when the Lord
metes out to everyone on Judgment Day
    the harsh chastisements they shall have earned with
        their hard-
heartedness? In our foolish pride we think
our lives secure, never suspecting a sword
    hangs by a thread over our heads. In a wink
death can take the strongest of us, pluck
him up and drop him into the darkness of ink
    in which is inscribed his destiny. Thunder-struck
he shall confront his God, who in life protected
mankind from madness, gave gifts he thought were luck,
    taught him right and wrong, and in love corrected
his repetitive lapses. I write this in chagrin,
knowing how many times I have neglected
    my conscience and duty, committing sin after sin.
I have bowed down before idols and worshipped the wood
of the rude trees that sported a manikin,
    have forgotten Jerusalem, my right hand, and good
and evil—although in my heart was another prayer,
that I hoped, Señor, you heard and understood,
    the mute but sincere devotion of my despair.

There were many like me who in prudence, or call it fear,
never observed your laws or would forswear
　　　their faith with religious fervor, but into the ear
of the Holy Office some informer would utter
the dread accusation, anyway. Called to appear,

　　　and forbidden the light of day, they learn to mutter
what snatches from our prayerbook they could recall,
their flavor now on the tongue both sweet and bitter.

　　　Their tears, one would think, would soften the heart of all
mankind, but it does not happen so. The fierce
inquisitor represses whatever small

　　　measure of pity he must have had once, turns worse,
and rejoices in his victim's torments. (Meanwhile,
he confiscates what was in the unfortunate's purse.)

　　　One learns to live by stratagem and guile.
⌐Though some, disgusted, convert or are suicides,
the rest of us try to imagine a domicile

　　　in a land of our own someday where peace abides
with plenty and where our children's children may grin
at griefs that are past as piety presides.

They shall no more be forced to commit our sin
of idol worship; the Ark will be restored;
and the gentiles, who will acknowledge that they have been

　　　outrageous, will allow us to worship the Lord
and bless him as we have been commanded to do.
That primate with the keys whom we have abhorred

　　　for his tyrannies will be exposed. What the Jew
knows, the world will acknowledge in regret,

6

and we shall emerge from this valley of death to view
　　Zion's hill once more with eyes that are wet
with tears that will be of joy./You weeping women,
dry your eyes and be brave, for we may yet
　　be restored to those ancient glories the Roman
destroyed and desecrated. The sacred flame
will burn again in the Temple. Say "Amen"
　　and believe the words of the prayer. Have faith in God
who will do this not for our sakes but for his,
as he has done before. Remember! Be glad,
　　for mercy is in his nature, and therefore this
anguish of ours, aberrant, cannot endure
for long (although in Heaven's view, what is
　　an instant seems an aeon here). What's more,
the gentile sees our pain, calls out to us,
"That God whom you believe in does not care . . .
　　or has he gone away?" Opprobrious,
he insults our helplessness. And if we dare
pray to you, it must be in secret. Does
　　our silence make it an unacceptable prayer?
We are hauled away to dungeons, tortures, death,
but worse than any of these, and harder to bear
　　is that apostasy they want. We all are loath
to sin but cannot atone in proper form
and are frightened both of praying and your wrath.
　　Whence cometh our help? Where is that mighty arm
with which you saved us once? We whisper the story
to children who have heard too much of harm
　　and can scarcely credit what we report of your glory.

But a day will come when the lesson is made as clear
on the dark slate of the world as it is in the starry
  firmament. Then will Christians learn our fear,
for you will smite them: along with their death râles
our prayers of thanks and praise will be what they hear
  in their final moments, and we shall hold festivals
to celebrate our deliverance and praise
your anger and love, which are reciprocals
  in your divine accounting. In those days,
your holy Name that has been obscured will shine
to dazzle once again in the noontide's blaze,
  and those who out of weakness might have inclined
toward sin will bend their knees before you and feel
the prophylactic awe that men who are blind
  must know when, by a miracle, they heal,
can see again, and blink in their remorse
for having doubted what their eyes reveal
  of the beauty of creation—which we, of course,
knew all along, though we may suffer now
from regulations priestly goons enforce.

  As we leave this life, they make us disavow
our faith and any hope of heaven's rest.
The best we can imagine is that somehow
  our torments, undeserved and unredressed,
may cease as we plummet into the deep abyss.
It may be that our martyrs will be blessed,
  and the ragged shrouds of their anabasis
be transformed into robes of cloth of gold,
as they are welcomed into eternal bliss.

Joy upon joy, a hundred-thousand-fold,
is the right reward for constancy of faith.
I believe in that golden heaven and am consoled
        to think that the prayers we recited under our breath
may have been heard and our forgetfulness
forgotten. The fire is hot, and in it your wrath
        may melt as all our sinfulness like dross
is cleansed away. What's left, thus purified,
will be like the finest gold which you will bless.

        That soul, cut off, abandoned, and denied
you will retrieve, for its sake and your own.
Thrice happy, such a one, close by your side,
        will celebrate the glory of your throne.

The Poem of Queen Esther

Describing the Monarchy of Ahasuerus, the grandeur of his opulent house, the banquet and the guest list, how he ordered Queen Vashti to appear, her disobedience, his vow in response to this refusal, and the law generally established on this subject.

To accomplish the lofty aims of your holy scheme,
you work, O Lord, in grand and terrible ways.
To you, as is only right, your creatures arise
to sing and become the instruments of your praise.
It is not presumptuous to ask to be
inspired so that your voice may sound in me.

The coal of my soul's ardor for you burns
me clean and I am faint, ecstatic, hot . . .
but the fountain of your compassion cools and soothes
so that I can bear that glory I do not
begin to deserve. You help me understand
the difficult enterprise I take in hand.

Into my spirit's murk, your bright light shines;
it is your voice that sounds in my throat, Lord,
as I undertake to celebrate that Queen
who long ago saved Israel from the sword,
a glance of whose beautiful eyes, appealing and sweet,
kept our blood from spilling onto the street.

In the city of Shushan there once lived the great
Ahasuerus, of Cyrus's line, a king
who reigned over many far-flung territories
that bowed to him in deference and would bring
him tribute: India's gold and Africa's treasure
heaped up in Shushan, wealthy beyond measure.

A hundred provinces he governed. Of these
no fewer than twenty-seven were his own
conquests, within the short three years in which
he had been sitting on his kingdom's throne.
The Jews had been vanquished seventy years before
by his forebear Nabucodonozor,

that potentate who had pillaged the holy Temple
of all its rich decor. What Jerusalem
had lost now ornamented the royal palace.
When the King had guests, he liked to dazzle them
with all his sumptuous loot, the many rare
and sacred objects hanging everywhere.

Look at those precious stones! See how they shine,
so that the sun looks dull beside them. Behold
the workmanship of the pieces, the elegance
with which those clever Jews could work in gold.
For the entertainments he puts on at night
their luster makes the evenings noontide bright.

Inlays of mother of pearl with an iridescent
sheen that tricks the eye as if it were born
in the sun instead of the depths of the sea beguile
the spirit with their changing hues that adorn
the halls of this sybaritic potentate
to tell the world that his power and honor are great.

The Zodiacal houses, the moon's phases, the sun's
seasonal track incised on the ceiling proclaim
creation's glories, for which he takes his share
of the credit, for is he not master of all? His fame
extends as far as the sun's span in the sky,
And in all their hundred tongues, his subjects cry

their praises and offer their prayers to him. He smiles
and gives a languid, perfunctory wave. He invites
le Tout-Shushan to come to his banquet pavilion
and stroll in his palace gardens. For seven nights
and seven days the world throngs there to admire
with an awe of which he seems never to tire.

Worked in the noble metals and precious stones
are scenes of war and peace, and each lunette
along the walls glitters with jasper, marble
and porphyry. A sunrise and sunset
at opposite ends of the great reception room
adorn, impose, and, if one may say so, loom.

On the doors, in bas-relief in sheets of brass
is a frontispiece or, one might say, book-plate
where the arms of the royal house are on display,
weapons and beasts, the heraldic devices great
houses choose for themselves (and every guest
seeing these emblems has to be impressed).

By day, the windows refract and chandeliers
reflect in their crystal lusters the light of the sun;
at night there is candlelight and everywhere
such sparkling of bright jewelry that one
has to take care to shield his eyes from the glint
of rubies that, head on, could make him squint.

Niello tesselations adorn the floors
except where the silken carpets hide them. On high,
sapphires hang from the ceiling here and there
scattered at random like stars that shine in the sky.
But none of this glitter and grandeur at every side
distracts the eye from the throne, the monarch's pride

with its hangings of silk and cloth-of-gold and gems
encrusting every surface. The royal chair
depicts the cities, mountains, rivers, and fields
of the kingdom on which the King is sitting there.
Minuscule armies in battle array recall
his triumphs and his enemies' downfall.

On the other side is a tiny vessel, its prow
seeming to make a wake of unequal waves
as it plies a cloisonné ocean. One can feel
the treacherous cross winds its captain braves:
it fills his bellied sails, but at the helm
he knows that at any time it can overwhelm.

In the banquet hall, the table, too, is worked
in intricate designs of ebony
and ivory that show the various foods
from all the provinces and, from across the sea,
from foreign lands, those dainties—spices, rare
fruits, and peculiar liquors they brew there.

No bird that flies in the air, or beast that lurks
on a mountain fastness or in some desert waste
or fish that swims in the sea that is not sent
to Shushan for its interesting taste.
The King can wave to his seneschal and grin,
and offer his guests . . . "More potted pangolin?"

From the chimneys in the cookhouse there arise
astonishing aromas better known
in Araby or Finland or the lands
beyond the Indus, making passers-by groan
in ecstasy at these hints of how good,
how lucky it is, to share the emperor's food.

The servants clear, and there, one sees, inlaid,
the representations of huntsmen with their snares
at the ends of the earth and others with sharp spears,
pursuing the quarry the kitchen staff prepares.
One senses the awesome power the ruler wields
over the earth that all this profusion yields.

It is not, after all, a question merely of catching
the fish or birds or beasts, but these must be
brought back on highways the royal engineers
have built and the army patrols to keep them free
of brigands and thieves, for wealth, by itself, is vain
unless there is order the king's men can maintain.

There are battle scenes as well, representations
of the men at the frontier whose brazen shields
thunder from the enemies' blows: their swords
reply like lightning on those battlefields.
Such storms are not uncommon out at the border,
but they subside again to peace and order.

By the will of the King or even his whim, these things
are set in motion and regulated. His hand
makes a small gesture and orders are cut with effects
as complicated and distant as they are grand.
That hand now raises a goblet to his lips.
He sniffs the wine's bouquet, approves, and sips.

An odd idea crosses his mind—that these
his guests, the assembled luminaries might
be even more astonished if the Queen
were to venture forth from the *haremlik* this night,
and show herself to them, his richest treasure,
his love, his heart's delight and his body's pleasure.

An all but unimaginable idea,
but he has imagined it and is bemused,
for what can he not do? What rules should he
obey, who makes the rules? A bit confused
by the drink, perhaps, and the company, he sends
the eunuchs to summon Vashti to join his friends.

She refuses of course. She can scarcely believe he means
for her to obey or to show such disrespect
to her, his wife, his Queen. Is this a test?
She sends back that refusal he must expect.
Or else, if he is serious, then she chooses
not to comply. At any rate, she refuses.

The King, enraged, embarrassed, sputters and fumes
at this defiance and scarcely believes his ears.
The empire's very foundation is compliance,
its obedience to his every wish. He fears
what may befall if such behavior is not
punished severely. Is it perhaps a plot?

He is fuddled with wine, but still it seems quite clear
that something must be done, for the kingdom shakes,
and in every household wives, hearing this news,
will rebel against their husbands—for whose sakes
he must now act. He must let the Queen be made
an example to all. And let them be afraid.

His advisors are divided, some supposing
that power must be maintained, and others urging
that justice, too, is important, and proper procedure.
The King, displeased, suggests that they may be verging
on insolence. Or even treason. He
wants counselors who know how to agree.

They back and fill, and bow and scrape, and confess
that their collective judgment has been affected
by their habit of servitude. They are too cautious
and grateful, all the more, to be corrected.
"Your majesty is always right," concedes
Memucàn, a prince of the conquered Medes,

who has learned in his captivity to serve.
"Power," he says, "must always make itself known;
only weak rulers rely on reason and justice.
The measure by which men judge a monarch's throne
is its arbitrariness. The question 'Why?'
allows debate and invites men to defy

their King's commands. Fear is a truer guide,
and kinder, too. What men cannot refuse
or argue with they learn at last to accept
obediently, and therefore you must use
your power to maintain it. Not even the Queen
can defy you, or at least must not be seen

to do so as your subjects watch. The royal
will can never bend. If you are the King,
the Queen must bow to you and must obey
her lord and master. It is no little thing,
for if you let this pass, and this be known:
then you shall have a diminished crown and throne.

The Medes' and Persians' law on this is clear—
that the queen must be put by, allowed to live,
but sent away somewhere into seclusion
and there must be a new queen who will give
the world a better example and obey
her husband in all things and in every way.

Your empire is great, your majesty.
Throughout the world all men respect and fear
your name and pay you tribute, but such honor
as you extract from satrap and emir
will not endure if that respect abates,
for hiding in every shadow treason waits."

The courtiers all applaud and the King nods.
But this is a serious matter: he does not smile.
He steers a difficult course, against the tide
of his feelings and close to reason's wind. Meanwhile,
his counselors avoid one another's eyes
as, in suspense, they wait and temporize.

The King is compelled by his own power to do
what he does not want. He cannot help but hate
that pomp of which he is prisoner, that wealth
that leaves him poor and needy. For reasons of state,
he does what he must. He sighs, he nods again,
and he signals to one of the clerks to fetch a pen.

⚬⚬ ▆◆▆ ⚬⚬

The lament of the King at Vashti's absence; the search through-
out the provinces for attractive virgins from among whom he
can choose a new Queen; the King's approval of the selection
of the kinswoman of Mordecai, Esther's cousin; her virtue and
beauty; how she was chosen and how she reigned; the warn-
ing of Mordecai to the Queen of those who were plotting to
kill the King; proof of the conspiracy; the punishment of the
conspirators; and the loyalty of Mordecai as inscribed in the
official records.

The flames of passion that once burned in the King
have turned to ashes now. His heart is cold
and its sweet balm is bitter. He is enraged
to be subject thus to vicissitudes his gold
cannot prevent. If anyone can fall,
even from thrones—what help are they at all?

He'd loved her, but that only makes it worse,
and he imagines her in some lush garden
grieving for him and expecting that any moment
a messenger may arrive with the royal pardon
policy and his pride keep him from sending.
Their matching torments seem to have no ending.

His solitude is his companion now,
and sorrow is there to greet him when he wakes
and attend him in the evenings when he retires.
Sometimes he feels desire in which he takes
a rueful pleasure—that this is what he deserves,
a protest from his body and its nerves.

In his orchard he can hear the turtledoves
rehearsing the refrains of their regret
out in the rain and wind where he would go
to join them if it weren't cold and wet.
Can nature be sympathetic? Does that make sense?
Or is it no more than pure coincidence?

He is befuddled, confused, and understands
that his mind isn't right. He cannot trust his own
emotions and reactions. Or anyone else's.
And overwhelmingly he feels alone
and even frightened, although he does not dare
let anyone at court guess his despair.

The silence he must maintain builds up inside him
a kind of pressure, a silent scream of pain
he cannot believe will not erupt. At last,
as he feels he is on the verge of going insane,
a numbness comes upon him, not the release
he thought he'd needed but, still, a kind of peace.

"What good are power and gold?" he asks. "What good
is anything, if I am thus diminished?
My love has turned to chagrin and I am king
of emptiness and sorrow. I am finished
with royal pomp, for life to me is vile.
It is not the Queen but I who am in exile.

The sun has fled from the sky, and night now reigns
always and everywhere. With beauty gone,
anything I look at is dull and gray,
and I am ruined by that which I have done,
myself. The empty corridors accuse
my folly, and I have nothing left to lose.

I go to bed alone now on chaste sheets
from which I chased the woman who was my bride,
faithful and modest always. What was I thinking?
I was beguiled by bad advice and pride
which now I brood upon in shame, and yet
it cannot be changed. I seethe in my regret.

My kingdom shrinks to this one doleful thought,
and I am become a vassal to my pain.
My courtiers are ghostly presences
I barely notice, locked inside my brain
as if in a dungeon, and I do not grant
that clemency I beg of myself. I can't.

I envy simple tradesmen in the streets
and even peasants, who are, compared to me,
happy in their lives, for their desires
are subject to their wills, and they are free
as I can never be. The joys they feel
are small and simple perhaps, but they are real."

His manner in the palace arouses concern
lest grief should turn to madness and endanger
the empire. The courtiers confer,
worried that his behavior grows ever stranger.
They agree what must be done: either they find
another queen, or the King may lose his mind.

Maidens from every province they will seek,
blondes and brunettes, slender or buxom, whatever
the King may find attractive. The decree
is put before him. He says that he will never
sign it, but he does, for they are clever,
and tell him the throne demands it—for its pride
would be offended, left unoccupied.

The girls arrive, weeping, giggling, silent,
lavishly dressed, or simply clad, but each
receiving from Hegai, the harem keeper,
a welcome and the rules that he must teach
his charges, one of whom will graduate
to majesty as Ahasuerus' mate.

A captive Jew there is in Shushan of
the line of Kish. Mordecai is his name,
the son of Jair, whose father was Shimei.
The family are of Benjamin's tribe and came
from Jerusalem: that memory he keeps
enshrined in his heart and every night he weeps.

He has an orphaned cousin he has reared,
Esther, a girl of striking beauty, grace,
and virtue. She is the solace of his life
of exile that is gentled by her face
and its serene expression. Like the sun,
she warms the world and dazzles everyone.

Her eyes, those windows of the soul, are full
of understanding, kindness, and a rare
compassion. When she raises them heavenward
in a fervor of humility and prayer,
simply to be near her is a gift—
a flower from which the sweetest perfumes drift.

Her lips are like that blossom's inner petals,
delicate, soft, and of a subtle hue
roses might envy, and her smile can gleam
brighter than the pearls one compares it to.
Have you ever, in a meadow at dawn, felt bliss
at its perfection? Esther's is like this.

As dawn restores the colors of the world's
dark canvas so that objects everywhere
seem to have undergone a new creation,
so by her casual glance can she repair
the prospect that an injured soul has seen
as barren waste to fertile, rich, and green.

That gold braid of the formal court regalia
cannot disguise the baseness of those who wear
their gaudy costumes. None of that vain show
compares in splendor to that of the real world where
the sun shines gold in a sky of royal blue—
the colors of creation's retinue,

to which, sometimes, snows add their ermine trim.
This panoply illustrates the holy book
wherein are written laws that have a beauty
no eye can compass. Only the mind can look
on such magnificence in transitory
glimpses that are Zion's pride and glory.

The hints of all this richness in Esther's eyes,
the King's commissioners see at once. They are
stricken, as they are sure their master will be
when she stands before him and he can gaze at her
as they do now. This beautiful young woman
who touches their souls . . . Can she be a mere human?

She looks to Mordecai for an indication
of what she should do. Her cousin, devout and wise,
wonders if this could be an intercession
of God, somehow a blessing in disguise.
Devout and humble, he tells her that she
must keep the faith and accept what is to be.

She is taken away and given over to experts,
cosmeticians, hairdressers, and those
enhancers of women's beauty. Couturiers fuss
and argue about her accessories and clothes.
What's right for her? What does the King like? What
may catch his eye, what color and what cut?

Mordecai, meanwhile, allows himself
to hope that this may turn out well for the Jews.
In hope and faith does a seed in the dark put forth
its shoots: the life and the light that it pursues
are the gifts of God. Can we trust any less
in the mercy of him whose holy Name we bless?

At length, the time arrives for Esther to be
presented to the Emperor. He waits.
They have reckoned to the second that degree
of suspense they can risk as he anticipates
the beauty they have found. His royal desire
they hope to spark and then fan into fire.

Her hair peeps out from a shimmer of cloth of gold;
her eyes burn from behind her veil of lace
like sea-foam the moon has silvered; and her gown
set with seed-pearls suggests her body's grace.
There are diamonds on its hem so that she seems
to float on a path of starlight and moonbeams.

Around her neck is a chain of intricate
design in gold, from which more diamonds shine,
as if, in the King's extravagant world of wealth
and luxury, she were part of the design,
or else, more modestly, implying that Esther
is entitled to such ornaments and luster.

But those are mere externals, artifice,
and easy enough to describe. Where is that pen
that can suggest her inner beauty the King
beholds or his transports few mortal men
have even dreamt of? But he is awake, and she,
amazingly enough, is as real as he.

No words will serve. Let us imagine rather,
the almost breathless silence of his awe,
humbled by the modesty and sweetness
with which she bore that majesty he saw
in her eyes and in the way that she could move.
He is dizzied as if falling—into love.

And she? Resigned to the celestial will,
she walks in faith upon the path of fate,
distracted neither by hopes nor fears, but steady
in her devotion. Whatever may await
will be at heaven's pleasure. How can she then
object or say a word—except "Amen"?

She does not envy and she is not proud.
Within her snowy bosom, there are no
such poisons flowing. Pious and serene,
she is at peace. Her thoughts and feelings flow
unrippled in those channels that her soul
has ordered for them, virtue its only goal.

To the throne room's grandeur she is all but blind,
for her eyes are fixed upon the greater glory
that nothing in this world can hope to match.
The splendors here are poor and transitory
compared to those. She seems to deign to grace
the great hall by her presence in this place.

He is delighted both by her and by
the novelty of finding something true
and fine to which he can aspire. Kings
hear flattery all the time from a retinue
of liars, rogues and fools, and soon become
distrustful—even paranoid—and glum.

Picture a turbulent sea where furious winds
whip the towering waves into a churning
fury, and then, suppose some tranquil depth
where there is silent stillness. The King is yearning
for that repose and respite: equipoise
is what he craves, not busyness and noise.

He sees it in her, feels his heart fly forth,
a moth drawn to a candle, as its wings
grow gorgeous, for the fire makes them glow
brighter and then singe as passion brings
that *Liebestod* for which it was intended,
fulfilled at the same moment it is ended.

A wedding, then, in the tenth month of the seventh
year of his reign, and she, his Queen, will sit
beside him on the jeweled throne to reign
and be admired, beautiful, exquisite,
and gentle. He is so happy, he relaxes
the rules for the payment of some provincial taxes.

He sends, in her name, gifts to the nobles and food
and clothing for the poor. He does her honor
in every way he can think of to invite
the empire to love her too and dote upon her
as he does, for that beauty, grace, and rare
goodness in her that he wants the world to share.

But who are her people? Who is she? His bride,
his wife, she is a stranger, nonetheless.
Where does such perfection come from? She
evades his questions, somehow. "Let him guess,"
her cousin has counseled her, "and you will whet
his appetite for what he cannot get."

Two eunuchs of the court, there were, Bigthan
and Teresh, who conspired against the life
of Ahasuerus, but Mordecai overheard
and revealed their plot to his cousin, who was the wife
of the King, to whom she conveyed this information.
He launched, forthwith, a thorough investigation.

They'd spoken in the Tarsic dialect?
But Mordecai, a linguist, had understood
what they'd been saying. Guilty, then, as charged!
The two were taken out to a nearby wood
where they were impaled, alive, on a tall tree.
For treason, this is the Persian penalty,

for evil must be punished, that those who think
of plotting so against the government
may be discouraged. Let them quake in fear,
envious, spiteful perhaps, but impotent,
and let it be recorded for all time
that such was the dire result of their vile crime.

— ⚏⬩⚏ —

The elevation of Haman and his pride; the scorn of Mordecai
and his refusal to humble himself before Haman; the hatred
Haman conceives and his plan to destroy all the Jews; his re-
quest to the King that every Jew in his kingdom be executed;
his offer to the King of ten thousand talents of silver if that
order be given; the King's accession to this request; and the
distress in the city as the decree is promulgated.

For our present pain, we like to believe, the divine
physician has his potent cures prepared
and keeps them ready for the woes he sees
his people face, that Israel may be spared.
What hateful Haman conceived then in his mind
offended heaven and all of humankind.

33

Promoted now, he stands beside the King
in a place second only to him in power
and honor. In such rare air does virtue grow,
or evil can put forth its baneful flower.
With a lack of limitation, a man can feel
a giddiness as if only he were real,

and the world is nothing but his dream or nightmare.
Let all bow down to him; let men agree
that nothing else and no one else can matter,
for they are slaves and agents, and only he
has any independent will. His word
is law, and others' babble is absurd.

On the court's turbulent ocean, Haman sails,
a proud vessel careening against the force
of buffeting winds that do not obstruct but serve
instead to hasten him further along his course.
If he hears moans and shrieks from high in the stays,
to his delighted ear they are hymns of praise.

He glows with the King's esteem, and the world,
    impressed,
caters to his every whim. Great men
hover about him, while lesser ones in need
turn to him as a magnetized needle when
you let it float will point to the pole star. He
is that fixed point in the skies of cupidity.

He comes to assume that such behavior is right
and proper and merely what he deserves. He grows
accustomed to hearing himself addressed in prayers
that he could grant in an instant if he chose—
or not, for either way his power seems
to have made the empire subject to his dreams.

The courtiers bow as low before him as
before their emperor or their god. In this
offense to heaven he takes outrageous pleasure.
That something in their behavior—or in his—
is blasphemous never crosses his mind at all
or that, given enough time, such pride must fall.

The only man who appears to have no fear
(or hopes of gain from Haman's fickle favor
that can produce the same servility)
is Mordecai, whose heart seems not to quaver
at Haman's scowls and frowns, however black.
In bland assurance, Mordecai stares back.

What is this grandeur after all but a writ
signed with a bird's quill and light as a feather?
If Haman banks and soars in an updraft now,
the sky in which he flies is God's, and the weather
may change as shifting winds bring clouds that dim
the sun so that the heavens may frown at him.

He watches as the counselors strut and preen
to reassure one another how they are as great
and good as they are wise and deserve that wealth
by which the gods acknowledge and validate
what the Emperor has decreed, the extravagant claims
implicit in all those titles before their names.

He is not blinded by this glitter whose eyes
are fixed on the much brighter eternal light
of the holiness of the law he trusts and loves
and, when called to account, the Israelite
is foolish enough—or brave enough—to declare
that the power and glory he worships are elsewhere.

"I am no ingrate," he says. "I am not disloyal,
but ever mindful and grateful for those rich
rewards I have received: my life, the world,
its wealth of wonders, and all the beauty which
my eyes behold are my creator's grand
gifts, more fine than man can understand.

I praise the Lord who made the universe
and is its master. In his hand is set down
on the slate of my heart his holy Name that time
and change cannot erase. His is the crown
of glory I worship, honor, and revere
more than that of an emperor or vizier.

How can I, after contemplating such
heavenly splendors see your poor displays
of pomp and ceremony and be impressed
or dazzled? How can they deserve my praise?
How should I fear your power, which is small
compared to that of the Lord who is master of all?

The vicissitudes of life on earth are merely
shadows that pass as the clouds fly by in the sky.
Above them, the sun still shines, and heaven reckons
rewards for our suffering here that, by and by
we'll have: for death, eternal life; for this
torture, an unimaginable bliss.

The kingdom of the Lord is good, and we
who know this are forgetful. Like the blind
we stumble along the road, confused, in flight
from what we cherish, leaving that behind.
We bubble up like fountains but then fall back
to seek the lowest level and make a track

of rivulets in the mud in which we settle.
How pitiable this is. Yet there are some
proud men who will congratulate themselves
and preen as if good fortune could not come
undone in an instant to be succeeded by
a wretchedness that lasts for eternity.

If I can glimpse, behind the billowing curtain
of the world's appearances, some indication
of what is worthy of worship, real, and true,
how can I bend my knee in subjugation
to mere shadows? Belief in fantasies
is childish or a symptom of disease."

Like a wounded lion, bellowing and roaring
from the spear that has struck his side and gives him pain
at every step, Haman groans and shouts
which only distresses him further. Nearly insane,
that lion worries the spear shaft but it hurts
him all the worse as more and more blood spurts.

Having suffered this blow to his pride, his soul
snarls and snaps in rage and he aggravates
the wound that causes him further torment. He glares,
and plans his revenge against the man he hates,
to inflict that hurt a hundred, a thousand fold,
the thought of which will make the blood run cold.

Can his luck have deserted him? Is this a sign
of worse to come? How can he tolerate
such insolence? He has not changed, nor has
the world. He must somehow obliterate
this blemish to his honor and self-esteem.
Carefully, he formulates his scheme.

The death of a single man is not enough,
is hardly proportionate to the offense.
He broods, fanning the embers of his hatred
into a fire, blazing and intense.
Nothing less than a holocaust will do:
let Mordecai die and all his people, too.

"How does your majesty allow," he asks,
"an alien element here who do not observe
your laws but keep their own? How can you let
such insolence go unpunished? They do not serve
your majesty but a god they cannot see.
They defy you and they live! How can this be?

When mists arise to obscure the sovereign sun
enthroned in the sky, its nature is to turn
the heat of its displeasure for that presumption
upon the offending vapors which then burn
away: with all its majesty restored
the sun shines all the brighter, afterward.

Without the blade of the sword and the fire's tongue
to inspire that fear by which the stiffest necks
must bend, there is chaos, sedition, treasonous plotting,
and all those other errors force corrects.
The good will of the people is all very well,
but a demonstration of force will better compel

correct behavior, here in the capital city,
and out in the provinces where rumor runs
with reports of the dire punishments that follow
insult or disobedience—anyone's.
Harshness is not in your nature, but you may find
it gentler, sometimes, than being kind.

If it may please your majesty," he says,
"let what I urge be done. Let them be killed
and their offense be punished, and I will give
as baksheesh, when my request has been fulfilled,
ten thousand quintals of silver that I will weigh
with my own hand to celebrate that day.

Publish throughout the realm a proclamation
condemning them, without exception for
their age or gender, to be put to death.
Your edicts and statutes must not be flouted or
ignored by those who choose to follow their own
laws and defy your majesty and throne.

Such an act will do your government good
enforcing complete compliance and catching up
those who drink from your bounty, having just sipped
forbidden liquor from their own dirty cup—
It is unclean, and a breach of manners, too.
Corrected, the world will approve of what you do."

He is done, and the King's impulse is to applaud
the words of his vizier. But decorum requires
that he reply in measured words. He nods,
barely giving a hint of his passion's fire
as he proclaims, "Of your silver, I want none.
But here is my signet ring. Let it be done."

The King's scribes are summoned. The day is set
as the thirteenth of the month on which satraps
are to carry out the decree and kill the Jews
of every province. Any dereliction or lapse
of vigor shall be punished with no appeal.
With the signet, Haman affixes the royal seal.

The edict is promulgated, hard as iron
that thirsts to shed the blood of Jacob although
there has been no crime committed. Innocent men
cry out and women in plaintive voices and low
croon to their children. Now and then is a howl . . .
Of a victim? Or is it a predator on the prowl?

There are no exceptions, the paper says. The old
defenseless ones and the very young will be
rounded up, the men and the women together.
Who can imagine such a catastrophe?
And how can the world permit such a dreadful thing?
But it's there in black and white, with the seal of the king.

To north and south, to east and west the soldiers
ride to deliver these sentences of death.
An eerie hush falls over the land as if
nature, itself, astonished held its breath
at Haman's grotesque decree. The people, too,
are stunned by what he has said he is going to do.

◦—◦ ▰◆▰ ◦—◦

In which is told the affliction of Mordecai hearing the news;
his Dream and his Lamentations when he covered himself with
sackcloth and ashes; his request to Esther that she try to change
the King's mind; her struggle with her fears about approaching
the King uninvited, which was a capital crime; the delibera-
tions of Mordecai; and at the end, the outcome of his fasting.

The appalling news that has filled the air at last
reaches Mordecai's ear to assault his spirit.
The flame in the lamp of his life's altar gutters
as he wails in profound lament. To overhear it
would break your heart! And rage is mixed with his dread.
Sackcloth he wears, and ashes are on his head.

In dreams he has been warned that there is danger
and that Israel has deeply offended heaven
by bowing down in public to worship Nabuco's
false gods and forgetting themselves even
at home where they ape Ahasuerus' refined
taste for *trayf* dainties. Clear in his mind

42

he can see the tempest approaching to shake the earth
and strike into every person's heart the fear
he felt himself as he watched dream dragons fighting—
a baleful omen it was, to see and hear
their charging, rearing, roaring and low hiss.
A sensible man would have run away from this,

but he couldn't move: one cannot escape the truth,
and he recognizes this as the world's way,
for this is Israel's life-and-death battle, and he
is one of those cartoon dragons in that dream fray,
the other, of course, being Haman, crafty, strong,
and proud. And their combat dragged on all night long.

The worst part of the battle: all around,
in the devastated terrain innocent creatures
suffered and died. But that weakness can be oppressed
is one of the sad lessons scripture teaches,
which is why it is difficult not to despise this life
of sorrow, iniquity, pain, and constant strife.

An unbearable scene, but then, somehow, a fountain
bubbled up from the earth to plash and play
and interpose between the combatants a brook
that grew to become a stream, a river, so they
could menace one another but do no more
harm. The riverbank then turned into the shore

of a mighty ocean with waves that came surging and
　　crashing
to hurl the sea spume high in the air to shine
in a dazzle of bright sunlight that covered the earth.
He has no doubt that this was a hopeful sign,
but what did it mean? To what person or thing
did the sudden interposition of that spring

refer? He is only half awake but concludes
that the sunshine represented his people's glory
so long obnubilated but never forgotten.
But what can he make of the rest of the allegory?
To whom can he look for succor and relief
having woken now to the real world and its grief?

The pity of it! The pain of Israel's people
makes him cry out in the stillness of the night,
and his groaning ascends to heaven. It is as if
his spirit has already passed on, for his fright
is not for himself but only his fellow Jews
whom the other nations persecute and abuse.

"Oh, you children of Jacob," he calls out, "see
how for your grievous sins are punishments sent.
You must bow your necks beneath a foreign yoke
who would not bow your heads in prayer. Repent
and pray to the Lord! Remember Zion's splendid
gifts and weep to think that they are ended.

The loss of your lives is a trifling thing. Far worse
is the Lord's loss of his people. For your neglect
of his eternal Wisdom you must pay,
and in his holy love, he will correct
our spirits' deficiencies. These hostile nations
are doing his bidding, imposing these tribulations.

It pains me, nonetheless, to see your anguish.
To live in exile, as we must do, among
a hostile people is worse than martyrdom.
We dream of what we were and tell our young
children of Zion's days of glory when
we used to dwell in peace. In the Temple then,

on the Day of Atonement, the High Priest, all alone
would enter the sanctuary where only he
could pronounce the ineffable Name of the Living God,
appeal to him, and beg for clemency.
Which one of us would not much rather give
his life than have that place defiled and live?

But here we are, far from the sacred wall
that yet stands of the Temple. Our kings are dead,
and we are scattered over the earth like leaves,
each of us trying to hide his mortal dread
so as not to burden further kith and kin,
though each of us knows the sorry plight we're in.

Shushan delights in our misfortunes, gloats,
and blames us, so that they can take the credit
for their prosperity. They believe that they
must be the chosen people now and have said it
must be a sign of the Lord's displeasure that we
are powerless in our misery—or he

more likely doesn't exist. And which is the worse
proposition? But either way they rejoice.
Meanwhile, turning to you in whom we believe,
we recite your ancient prayers and they give voice
to our plea for mercy. Come, Lord, to the aid
of your children who are afflicted and afraid.

The sunshine of your love in which we basked
for countless generations is covered over
by a cloud; the tide has ebbed; and we are stranded
and pray for a wind to come that will uncover
that sun and for the floodtide's water to reach
our vessel's hull and free us from this beach.

You loved us once, protected us and made us
prosper. We can never forget those days,
and you, too, must remember how we offered,
instead of these complaints and dirges, praise
and prayers of thanks. Our antiphons would rise
from earth to resonate and fill your skies.

Those blessings are not gone from our repertoire.
All we need is the proper occasion when you
shall unsheathe your sword and liberate your servants
who are oppressed, as we entreat you to
for mercy's sake and honor's, but above
all, for the sake of your people whom you love."

So Mordecai says. He rises then from bed
and ventures forth to the palace. To contravene
the etiquette of the court and the King's laws,
he puts on his funereal gabardine,
for without a royal invitation, none
is permitted to approach or address the throne.

The royal proclamations having arrived
at the outposts of the empire, Israel cries,
puts on sackcloth and ashes, sits in mourning,
lamenting its condition to the skies,
and looking to heaven whence its help must come
from Haman's hatred and his opprobrium.

The Queen, meanwhile, has heard how Mordecai
sits in the antechamber where he wears
the paraphernalia of those who grieve the loss
of a loved one and recites a mourner's prayers.
She sends to know what hurt he has received—
to share it, if it cannot be relieved.

Her messenger returns with her cousin's words:
his wretchedness is not for himself but, worse,
for all the house of Jacob, Haman having
turned the King against them with his curse.
The edict has gone out, and everywhere
the Jews are terrified and in despair.

He explains the sad details, and Esther sees
what hurt Haman will cause her kinsmen—unless
she does as Mordecai asks and goes to the King
to appeal to his love, pity, and gentleness,
to retract his edict, for only he can give
the order that will let her people live.

But the King must send for her, as he has not
for thirty days now. Is his ardor cool?
Dare she go unbidden? Should she risk
her life that way by violating his rule?
It isn't fear for herself but, if she tries
and fails, what then? Will she not jeopardize

all Israel? She wrestles with this question.
Her desire is clear—to do what is right and good—
but how can her frail shoulders bear this burden?
Where can she find the strength and wit? Where should
she look for help and guidance? Has she a choice?
From deep in her soul, she hears an answering voice:

"Your life," it says, "is a part of your people's life.
You are not separate. Let the King know this—
that if he puts the rest of the Jews to death
he will, by that same order, execute his
own beloved Queen who shares that throne
on which he will remain to mourn alone.

Do not suppose a crown can keep you safe.
He cannot think so, either, who realizes
that to pardon one is to overturn the entire
edict: there can be no compromises.
There is either a law the soldiers are fulfilling
or else there is only so much random killing.

You could, of course, run away and save yourself,
but where would you go? And how could you bear the
    thought
of having failed your people? Bitter chagrin
would be your portion. Do as you know you ought,
whatever may be the outcome of your behavior,
as your father's child and, I hope, your people's savior.

You could perhaps do nothing, and try to pass
as a gentile, but it's a bitter life that awaits
those whose existence is fiction. At any moment
(which the impostor forever anticipates),
he may be unmasked. That self he has tried to deny
will return to life and betray him, and he will die.

Who can read the riddles of heaven? Why
were you picked out and promoted thus except
to serve God and your people? Can you refuse
your own fate? Heaven's hard bargains must be kept.
Trust in God, for He has entrusted you
with a sacred duty. What else can you do?"

Thus it says, and the Queen in her great anguish
has to accede to the force of its argument.
To prepare, she resolves not only to pray but fast
for three days and she makes known her intent
to Mordecai and asks that he invite
all Jews to pray with her, all day and night,

for her success, of course, but, failing that,
if she does not find favor with the King,
then for her soul's repose and the end of grief
which are the gifts that death is said to bring
to that narrow bed in which we all lie down,
the poor, the rich, and those who wear a crown.

Mordecai receives this word from the Queen
and hastens to comply with her request,
but the purpose of these prayers he does not declare
to everyone; he keeps this in his breast,
a secret. Nevertheless, it is understood
that these oblations must be for Israel's good.

The arrival of the Queen into the King's presence; the com-
passion of his welcome to her; his offer to her even of half the
kingdom; her invitation to the King and Haman to come to
her banquet; Haman's departure and Mordecai's disrespect;
Haman's consultations with his wife and friends and their
advice to him to build a gallows fifty cubits in height in the
palace courtyard on which to hang Mordecai.

Three days and nights of prayer and fasting follow
in which the Jews of Shushan implore the aid
of the Lord and his holy angels, that they embolden
Esther, their Queen, whom they know to be afraid:
"Please God, let her remarkable beauty find
a way to the King's heart and make him kind.

That holy light that existed before the sun's,
that aboriginal brightness of the creation
they try to imagine, knowing that what they see
is a pale shadow of that, an imitation,
but that power, being eternal, still can make
the darkness flee and blackest evil quake.

Rainbows of the covenant still adorn
the skies as the clouds break up, and there are flowers
in springtime in the meadows where the snows
covered the earth but a moment ago. Those powers
we take for granted are marvelous nonetheless.
Let them protect our good Queen whom we bless."

She ventures through the gate of the women's pavilion
and into the chambers of state and the throne room
   where
the King holds court and deals out life and death.
She tries to be brave and tells herself he will spare
her life . . . and she sees him smile. At her? At her fear?
At any rate, he signals for her to draw near.

She feels her strength return and allows herself
to hope. She sees the loving look in his eye
and feels a surge in her spirit of answered prayers:
whatever she asks, she knows the King will reply
in kindness and love—and therefore he will give
assent and allow her and her people to live.

And he? His bosom melts as his royal pride
dissolves into spontaneous boyish joy.
He forgets the jeweled scepter in his hand
as if it were a trifle, a mere child's toy.
His kingdom? An imaginary place.
Nothing is real to him except her face.

His tongue in his mouth cannot produce the words
his mind dictates. It lies there, useless meat.
He wants to declare his gratitude and love
to the vision who is kneeling at his feet
but rises at the gesture that he makes.
At last, after much effort, the silence breaks.

"O Queen," he says, "love of my life, my sweet,
I welcome you here in joy. I cannot express
the depths of my ardor. Instead, I invite you to ask
for anything, even half my empire. 'Yes,'
will be my answer, and I shall give with pleasure
that token of a love beyond all measure.

You are silent? Why? I yearn for you to speak!
I have raised you up and will lift you even higher
to soar in the sky on the wings of the god of love
that beat the air, a bellows to my desire.
You own me altogether: claim any part
of me and I shall give it with all my heart.

I look into your eyes and in them glimpse
what paradise was like, or heaven must be,
as the anguish of my soul eases and light
fills the dark spaces within me to let me see
there is good in the world, if only we could learn
how to recognize it at every turn.

All that I know of policy and statecraft
your gentle presence here in this hall impeaches.
I feel within myself a yearning for better
than what I have been. My torpid spirit reaches
upward, and I desire to make life worth
your praise. Ask of me anything on earth!"

Imagine a ship that pitches and yaws in the waves
of a turbulent ocean, but then, as the storm relents,
rights itself, as its sails fill and it glides
on a glassy blue, and you will have some sense
of Esther's settled spirit, as confidently
she plots her course on a now pacific sea.

"Your valor and worth," she says, "command the love
of all your people, but I, your wife and slave,
am closer, know you better, and therefore love
with greater fervor, seeing how generous, brave
and good you are. I rise, and yet I feel
my heart within me, reverent and grateful, kneel.

My life is yours, and every breath I take
is by your leave. All I can offer, then,
beyond what you already own, is awe
for you who are lord and master of all men
whom I address to thank, praise, and adore,
using the word I learned in my prayers: 'Señor.'

Your offer is magnificently kind,
but I would not diminish your wealth and might
by any jot or tittle. All I ask
is that you and Haman attend upon me tonight
at a supper or, say, a banquet I shall prepare.
It would delight me if you and he were there."

Hearing her words, the King is deeply moved
with love for his wonderful Queen. As absurdly small
is her request as her love for him is great:
she could have asked for anything at all
but didn't. His majesty grins from ear to ear
and gives his promise that both of them will appear.

That night the King renews his generous offer
and her request is that they should come again
for a second evening. Ahasuerus agrees
that they will sit down together once more. Then,
unsure of herself in what she has essayed,
she looks to heaven for courage, guidance and aid.

Whether it be through madness or too much drink,
or spitefulness—he is an Agagite—
Haman has threatened her people whom he means
to annihilate. And in her grief and fright
she has to entertain him. It is vile,
and yet she sits there and contrives a smile.

At the end of the evening, Haman is full of himself,
having been invited to see the Queen
which no other man in the empire could dream
of doing. He therefore cannot help but preen.
That Jew, he thinks, will learn respect for one
whom the King treats almost as if he were a son.

When he gets home, Haman fusses; he complains
how success and wealth are worthless unless mankind
acknowledge them and defer, as men should do,
if they are not insane or deaf and blind.
Mordecai's slight was trivial, that's true,
but annoying still, a pebble in one's shoe.

He complains to his wife, Zeresh, in whom he trusts
and in whom he has always found a sympathetic
ear. And he discusses with close friends
if Mordecai's faults be cultural or genetic.
They do not disagree. They have no doubt
that Haman is quite right to be put out.

"What does a man work for?" he asks. "And why,
having struggled to the top, should one permit
his achievement to be belittled and his whole life
dismissed or ridiculed? It is not fit
or right, I say. The social fabric frays
if the populace forgets respect and praise.

The Jew's affront is no mere personal matter,
for his insult to me also touches the King
who has preferred me among all his subjects
and confides and trusts in me for governing
his far-flung territories. For this reason
this is no social lapse but an act of treason.

How much gold is in the world? How many
rubies and diamonds? What do we pursue
but that share of wealth our efforts and luck deserve?
Should we then suffer insults from a Jew
who takes no notice of what we have in our purse
except perhaps to envy or to curse?

An empire is not merely territory
but a realm of the mind about which men agree,
complying not with force but just the threat,
the idea of force—as real as the fields they see
around them in which they labor every day
to earn their bread and the taxes they have to pay.

The power of law is no more than a dream
that everyone shares as we have learned to do.
Should the people be disturbed and rouse themselves,
anarchy would inevitably ensue.
A hanging every now and then prevents
the chaos that would be the consequence

of freedom of thought—or call it what it is,
a license to secede from the nation at large
and for every man to follow his own path.
Authority vanishes. No one is in charge.
What keeps the sun on its track or the moon in place?
Without rules, they would spin out into space!

The empire we may liken to a huge
creature of which I am the mind. At court
we receive its treasures, as a stomach takes in food
for the body's nourishment and its support.
The sun that gilds and the moon that silvers the earth
serve each of us according to our worth.

For you and me, the horde of the world's horrors
are turned to table dainties: beasts that reek
of blood from the hunter's spear or the fisherman's net
appear before us every night of the week,
reborn, as a phoenix is, in the cookstove's fire
to an elegance only connoisseurs can admire.

Such marvels are routine with us. A man
facing the executioner's rope or blade
I can, if I choose, retrieve, commuting his sentence,
and giving him life again, if he has made
an elegant apology I have found
amusing enough to want to keep him around.

When I am at court, the King endorses my actions
and even reflects my moods: if I am content,
he is as well; but if I am sad or angry,
he is as likely as not malevolent
and even cruel. It has been said that we
are as much alike as fruits from the same tree.

And the Queen who loves and adores her sovereign
    lord,
understands how close we are and she invites
me to attend with him at her soirées
and share in their familial delights.
Not by mere words do they proclaim my worth;
their public deeds make it known throughout the earth.

Glory, a living thing, must either grow
or else diminish. My share of it is great,
except for what that worm has besmirched, that Jew,
Mordecai, and it cannot tolerate
such an affront. A blot, it must be removed,
and he, as a warning to others, be reproved.

My reputation soars in the sky, a mighty
sea bird that seldom deigns to set foot on the ground.
I shall spread out my wings and fly again
when that irksome son of Judah is brought down
plummeting as we do in our worst dreams,
for having affronted one whom the world esteems."

His cronies, hearing Haman's complaint, agree
that once the cause is removed, the anguish stops.
The fruit of the gallows tree is often sweet
when, having come to ripeness at last, it drops
to stretch a neck that in life refused to bend
and bring the offense—and offender—to an end.

Haman's wife, perhaps taking her cue
from this suggestion, bows her head as she speaks
saying that all will be well. The King is friendly,
confides in him and trusts him. What he seeks
is for the common good. Knowing this, the King
will follow Haman's counsel in this small thing.

⊷ ⧫ ⊶

Unable to sleep, the King requests his ledger; reading in it the
account of the loyalty of Mordecai that has not been recog-
nized, he asks Haman how to reward extraordinary service;
Haman, believing himself to be the one the King wishes to
favor, replies to the King; Haman complains to his wife and
friends who have predicted his downfall; and Haman attends
at the second banquet.

It is late at night, and the King is feeling drowsy:
neither asleep nor fully awake, he turns
and tosses while his thoughts and dreams are dancing
in the shadows on the wall. A candle burns
in reassurance, but something he cannot name
is bothering him and causing him fear and shame.

What has he done? Or left undone? The thought
is vague but irksome. Something is amiss
and calls out to him, piteous and abject.
He has his sense of majesty but, this
disturbs it, as if he wore his crown askew.
How can he set it right? What can he do?

60

He calls for his great ledger. Let it be
brought so he can examine this account
of what's owed him and what he owes to others.
What troubles him may be some small amount,
for matters of great importance do not tax
the mind, while trifles fall between the cracks.

Attendants fetch the record book. The King
commands a clerk to open the volume and read,
giving the silent letters voice and life
to remind Ahasuerus of details he'd
forgotten but had kept there, stored away
where they might be retrieved in just this way.

Here, reduced in scale, is his empire,
its high mountains, its fertile fields, its coast
where the trading vessels come into port with rich
cargoes. In peace, his people prosper, and most
are grateful to him and therefore loyal, as he
lives up to their ideals of majesty.

But there are always ingrates and malcontents,
and he hears the recitation of how a plot
of treason was foiled by the efforts of Mordecai
who defended his King and country. "And was he not
rewarded?" his Majesty asks, almost by the way.
"How did we honor him?" "It does not say.

Nothing is written here in the book of acts."
For a moment, the King is silent. "How can this be?
Good government needs both punishments and rewards.
An omission of this kind is offensive to me.
My honor being involved in this, there must
be prompt correction made that is fair and just.

Open-handed with malefactors whom we
condemn to the dungeons to languish or to die
on the gallows-tree, should we not also be
forthcoming to those we love? Let us rectify
this lapse of manners and contradiction of
our wish to rule not only through fear but love.

The scepter in my hand is an elegant club
but rich with gold and jewels—it can destroy
in vengeance or can elevate and enrich.
One who wields it learns in time to enjoy
its range of powers: among them I can choose
which and when and for whom I will use.

The loftiest aims are worthless without a dreary
diligence and attention to small details.
That horde of clerks and ministers shuffling papers
looks impressive but, over and over, fails
and I am forced, myself, to do the work
as if I were some glorified chief-clerk.

Conspiracy, treason . . . These are what we imagine
behind every servile smile and compliment,
which does not mean they do not exist and menace
the empire with their sinister intent,
for which the only cure is that a few
good men are as loyal as Mordecai, the Jew."

As the King is seeing the glimmer of his idea,
light itself appears in the sky with the dawn
of a new day's miracle, figuring that first
day of creation. The darkness of chaos is gone,
and objects resume their places and shapes as the gloom
lifts and attendants and courtiers enter the room,

among whom there is Haman, whom the King
addresses, asking, "What would you suggest
I do for someone I felt inclined to honor
greatly and thank? What would he like best?"
Haman is pleased and deeply flattered, for he
infers that he is himself that honoree.

"Señor," he answers carefully, "your vassal
did whatever he did for love of his king
and needs no further reward than that he knows
you love him in return. The ideal thing
would be to deck him in royal robes. Let him lead
a parade through the streets, mounted on your steed,

with heralds proclaiming for all the world to hear,
'This is the man in whom the King delights
and whom he is pleased to honor.' Let him bask
in the warmth of the people's smiles. Nothing requites
better the service of one whose love and esteem
for you are the greatest. This would be like a dream.

And let the privy counselors walk behind him,
to signal by their presence that they agree
with what the herald announces—that they love you—
and concur in your judgment with unanimity,
lest anyone suppose that envy might
be lodged in some men's hearts with its foul blight."

The King, delighted, answers, "Very good!
The man I have in mind is Mordecai,
the Israelite. Let those rewards you have named
be given, and you can walk before him and cry
to all the people that this is a man who has won
his sovereign's love. Today, let this be done.

I am grateful to you as well for conceiving this
splendid idea. The people see displays
of the royal anger when traitors are put to death.
Let them see also how royal love can raise
even him who was lowest in their sight,
if he be loyal, to an unimagined height."

Think of a wild stallion and how it will buck
and rear and how it paws the ground with its hoof
and foams at the mouth in rage at the bit and bridle.
Haman, taking the King's words as reproof
to his proud spirit, wants so to protest,
but clenches his teeth in the silence he thinks is best.

He must disguise his arrogance and pride
so as to seem as humble and self-effacing
as anyone in the kingdom. Bowing and smiling,
he hides from the King and court how his heart is racing
as he reasons with himself: the worse the blow
the greater his revenge will be also.

His anger is a fire: he feels its heat
and a pressure that at every moment grows.
Repressing it, he fears he may explode,
as he cannot afford to do, he knows,
here in the King's presence: he must bite
his tongue and keep his smiling lips sealed tight.

How strange is the mind! He tells himself his pain
is something in which to take a kind of pleasure,
anticipating how the time must come
when he can impose it himself, measure for measure.
To soothe his humiliation he has the sweet
prospect of Mordecai's anguish in defeat.

Revenge and retribution are bitter fruits
that ripen slowly, and one must bide his time,
faithful as any lover or pious priest,
awaiting the expiation of the crime
that has caused the hurt he nurses, knowing in this
world and within his grasp is the hope of bliss.

He revels in his shame, for his chagrin
is merely an aperitif: the meal
is yet to come, an entré, bloody rare.
The idea has an exquisite appeal,
in contemplating which he shows a grin,
or rictus, that is pleasure's evil twin.

He passes on the royal command. The Jew
is summoned to the palace for the fête
the King intends for him. Haman goes home
in silence. Although this business is not yet
concluded, he is overwrought and seething.
Indeed, he has some difficulty breathing.

Smart as he is, he knows intelligence
cannot remake the world. No amount of thought
can rewrite by even an iota the King's
commandment, and the battle he has fought
to keep his spirits up is hopeless. He
gives way at home to an abject misery.

He groans and sobs; his curses mix with boasts.
But what is the good of enterprise and scheming
when, out of the blue, the mad whim of a king
can undo all and reduce to idle dreaming
a man's career? He moans to Zeresh, his wife,
that he is a fool and hates his wasted his life.

"The fire of my youth's ambition has flared
and died away, and nothing remains but ashes.
The honors I have earned all mock me now:
instead of the praise I'm used to, jeers and lashes
are my bitter portion. Helpless, we are tossed
on a vast ocean and don't even know we're lost.

I always knew that this was the lot of men
but believed myself to be different, a special case.
I had set my course and was making splendid progress,
but now the truth is staring me in the face.
The powerful waves of fortune break over my head
as I pitch and yaw and founder and wish I were dead.

Thoughts of retribution soar and glide
high above my head . . . and out of reach,
as if to mock me or demonstrate how small
my meager powers are, and I beseech
the gods of darkness of whom men are afraid
to acknowledge me their servant and grant me aid.

As in a nightmare, I await a blow
the pain of which I already feel. I want
to run but my muscles refuse to obey my mind's
commands and I am paralyzed and can't
escape. I try but cannot even scream.
And then I wake to a world worse than my dream.

All the pomp and grandeur I enjoyed
is a burden to me, and Mordecai's humble station
is a kind of weapon against which I have no
defense. I am the laughing stock of the nation.
What can I do? How can I bear it?" He ends
begging for answers from his assembled friends.

"If you do not believe in good," they say, "then trust
in evil, for fortune is fickle but often kind
to those who, like it, are harsh (or unsentimental).
Philosophers are fools, beguiled by the mind,
and cannot see their hands before their faces.
When every law is unjust, they are all hard cases.

The Hebrews are no cause for worry. Their nature
is to be hated and treated harshly. They fall
like motes of dust in the air, which is why they believe
they will also rise to that heaven on which they call
in the desperation that they are driven to.
But do we give credence to fantasies of the Jew?"

As Haman, alternating between his rage
and fear, worries and frets, the moment nears
of the Queen's second banquet. He cannot
fail to appear. He tries to conceal his fears,
playing his part the best he can—but they
have written, produced and even directed the play.

⋯⋯ ⊰✦⊱ ⋯⋯

The prayer of Queen Esther; the second banquet; the reac-
tion of the King when he is told of Haman's cruelty to her
people; his fury as he leaves to walk in the garden; Haman's
begging for his life of the Queen who has retired to her couch;
the King's return and his order that Haman's head be cov-
ered; and the description of the gallows Haman had caused to
be erected for Mordecai but on which he, himself, is hanged.

The Queen is deeply troubled, her grief and fear
warring within her as she carries out her plan:
having invited the King and Haman together
to a splendid supper, she will do what she can,
for she is that fountain of Mordecai's mystic dream.
God's mercy bubbles up in her heart in a stream,

as it did at the world's beginning back in the Garden
where its sweet waters flowed to neutralize
all sin, as it still can do, for it reconciles
conflict, nourishes hopes, and revivifies
their delicate rootlets. They put forth new blooms
that astonish the air with exquisite perfumes.

What can she do? Or, rather, inquire how
is the thing to be done? The means are clear and the goal,
and, putting aside the delicate questions of honor
and pride, there still remains her pristine soul,
unversed in and unaccustomed to feminine wiles
and the calculation of gestures, looks, and smiles.

She prays: "O Great and Eternal Being who
with a generous hand has bestowed upon us all
your gifts and mercies, like the sun that supports
life here on earth, I pray to you now and call
on you for protection not for my life but for
that of your people, who worship you and adore

although for their faith in you they are facing death.
In pity, let your holy Name descend
to earth to show its power and in the hearts
of cruel men strike awe. Once more, defend
your people from their blows and those that we
inflict upon ourselves in our misery.

We know only too well that we are unworthy,
having failed to keep your laws, and yet our yearning
for truth and goodness must count for something. The spark
of faith is still alive in us and burning
however dimly. The tongues of its hot fire
dance in the gloom, the beacons of our desire

for heaven. We may be weak but you are strong
and on your abundant patience we rely
and your compassion as deep as the infinite sea.
The stoniest heart must yield itself, by and by,
to the battering on it of your waves of grace
that offer redemption to even the hardest case.

If, from the scales of justice there is no
appeal, then which of us can doubt his fate?
For anyone here to rise, you must descend
and with a merciful thumb adjust, abate,
and mollify the findings of your fury.
Be advocate as well as our judge and jury.

Those enemies of Israel who oppress us
are not your servants; they are your enemies too,
perverting your righteous laws, but we imagine
there must be some explanation for what they do.
Is this perhaps a punishment we have earned—
to be imprisoned, tortured, and then burned?

It cannot be so, for you are a God of compassion,
and in loving-kindness will save us once again,
as you have done so many times before
from the cruel machinations of evil men.
Generations from now, we will tell the story
of how you preserved us and we will exalt your glory.

Use me as you used Jaël, once to smite
the mighty Sisera in her tent. I beg
to be your instrument as that brave woman
was who took her hammer and tent peg
and drove it into his skull. By what she dared,
were the Canaanites subdued and Israel spared.

The hardest of Egyptian hearts was forced
to acknowledge at last your majesty and might
as the wall of water that formed to let us pass
dissolved and drowned them all, and in the fright
of their final moments on earth, they understood
how evil's power is less than that of good.

To Pharaoh and then the Canaanites you displayed
a righteous wrath that surely you can repeat
in some impressive fashion, an intervention
by which you shall contrive again the defeat
of Israel's foe, for if you wished us ill,
I have no doubt that you would work your will

against us, yourself, as a loving father should,
punish your errant children, but wield the rod
with your own hand. Meanwhile, protect us from
those who have never acknowledged you as God
or prayed to you as our fathers did. Give aid
to Israel's children, suffering now and afraid."

She feels in her soul the calm of the ocean's depths
to which, nonetheless, a penetrating ray
of sunlight filters down. As if she were
a mermaid, she swims in grace. Fear floats away,
and she prepares for Haman and the King
with confidence of what the night will bring.

The three of them take their places at the great
festive table the Queen has prepared heaped high
with rare viands on golden platters. Servants
with crystal flagons of various wines stand by
ready to pour into each of their jeweled cups
and replenish whatever one sips as he sups.

"O Queen," says the King, "you own my heart. You are
the light of my chest, the breath of my eyes. In you
is all I desire, and what you want, I want.
My soul leaps up like a boy's and wants to do
something amazing to make you laugh aloud
in delight, or something noble to make you proud.

Your laughter is like the sparkle of morning dew
that freshens and revives the meadow to make
the flowers there for the moment what they'd be
in a perfect world, and through you, and for your sake,
I, too, am renewed in aspirations of
ruling my people well, in justice and love.

I see my life between your eyes; your mind
is where I want to live; your memory is
the heaven of my desire. In that splendor
of your regard I'd know celestial bliss
on earth, for all my happiness is there,
and praising you is my perpetual prayer.

If you could see into my soul, if my
chest were crystal, you could discern a small
image there of yourself above the altar
on which I dedicate in reverence all
I have and do and am, an offertory
I gladly make to your name and its glory.

If heaven in its wisdom were to enlarge
the extent and wealth of my kingdom, already wide
as a man can imagine, I should not be more happy
than I am now with you or take more pride,
for you are the kingdom of my soul, and I
live happily there. Without you, I would die."

"Señor," she says, "I understand the gracious
words you have spoken, feeling, I confess
that same devotion, the depth of which I cannot
fathom let alone begin to express.
I should rather be the giver but, for your sake,
accept with love, my lord, the offer you make,

and impose upon your majesty—for my life
is threatened. Bitter hatred, like a sword,
hangs over my head and those of all my people.
From this dire threat you can, with a single word,
deliver us. You wish my lord, to give
a gift? I beg then, let my people live.

Our enemy's malevolence has no cause
except bloodthirstiness. There is no good
in reasoning, then, or offering satisfaction,
when nothing will satisfy him but our blood.
In terror and dismay, my people cry
for justice, mercy, and reason. And so do I.

Unless you intercede, we are again
subjected to the galling yoke of the slave
who watches as his weeping children and frail
parents are dragged off and cannot save
them or himself. He is afraid, but, worse,
is his helplessness to do anything but curse

his enemies, the wicked world, the life
he leads in it, and even its creator.
From this despair you can save my people. Forgo
the blood money. Your wealth will be much greater
and your glory, too, for heaven is not blind
to deeds of goodness performed by humankind."

"Who is this wicked man?" the King inquires.
"Who threatens you? Who dares? Who thus incurs
my anger?" The scowl upon his royal face
is menacing indeed, and his heart stirs
in indignation that such a thing can be.
Esther points her finger at Haman: "He!"

The King, enraged, can hardly breathe. He rises
abruptly and hurries out of the room. He feels
in need of his garden's calm. Esther, meanwhile,
collapses onto a chaise longue. Haman kneels
before her to beg for mercy. Will she spare
his life? The King, returning, finds him there,

his hand clutching the fringe of her gown. "You are
    mad!
You presume to touch the Queen, to desecrate
the altar of my love?" the King exclaims.
"This is a sin nothing can expiate.
Your continuing existence affronts my eye
for which the cure is that, in a wink, you die."

That word has scarcely passed the Emperor's lips
when the guards seize Haman and cover his head with a sack
as is done with those condemned to death. His eyes
are as good as closed, and he confronts the black
and timeless void of his future in the grave.
"Quite right!" remarks Harbona, a eunuch slave,

"and by a neat coincidence, there stands
a gallows out in the courtyard he had built
for Mordecai against whom he had conceived
a violent detestation. For Haman's guilt
it offers itself, full fifty cubits or higher—
and to rise in the world has always been his desire.

Let him be hoist upon his own petard
to show the world what happens to those who pervert
the royal power, for he, who was your servant,
ought to have given help to your friends and hurt
those who'd offended you or given cause
for your dislike by violating your laws.

His only law was self-aggrandizement
and he was loyal to his own arrogance
more than he ever was to you. That gallows
is all you need in the way of evidence."
The King confirms the sentence: "For his guilt
let him die on the gallows that he built."

He turns to the Queen to comfort her, for she
was troubled by this man and his wicked threat
to Israel. She smiles in gratitude
but nervously, for she is unable yet
to emerge from the dark shadow Haman cast
or enjoy the freedom from fear of a peril past.

The King gives Haman's house and goods to the Queen, who gives them in turn to Mordecai who also receives the seal of state; the Queen asks that Haman's proclamation be repealed and the Jews be protected from danger; and it is decreed that the Jews may arm in order to defend themselves from those who threaten them and that they may enjoy the same freedom of worship as do gentiles to celebrate their festivals and worship according to their traditions.

The arrow of love that wounds can also heal,
destroying Haman utterly while saving
Mordecai's life. Queen Esther's gratitude
and joy are what the monarch has been craving,
the sweetest thing he can imagine. If she
is no more troubled, neither, then, is he.

All Haman's wealth the King bestows upon
the Queen to give her cousin Mordecai
to reward his loyalty and let him taste
a few of those good things that gold can buy.
He is grateful and delighted, not from greed
but because he can give help to those in need.

The ring with the royal signet that Haman wore
on his middle finger, Mordecai now wears
but not as the plaything of some naughty child.
He wants to use its power in men's affairs
for good, promoting justice and happiness
throughout the land and relieving their distress.

He wants to govern not through fear but love
and thereby win the hearts and minds of the nation,
and divine approval as well, for the sun will shine
on bountiful fields in sign of approbation
of the virtue that may be its own reward
on earth but in heaven strikes a responsive chord.

Meanwhile, the Queen implores her lord and master,
"Let me impose on your love with a further request—
that you rescind the wicked edict of Haman
against my terrified people, sorely distressed
although they have done no wrong. They look to you,
their only hope, who can, with a word undo

that grave injustice. Do this, not for me
but for pity's sake, and for your own soul's pleasure.
Extend your hand to those who reach out to you,
and grant them those gifts precious beyond all measure—
liberty and life, and with every breath
they will bless you, the monarch who rescued them
    from death.

That royal scepter you hold in your hand that was
a weapon can be an instrument of peace,
or a wand the wave of which can relieve my people's
pain when you order your soldiers and guards to cease
their persecution. You can end the fear
aroused in your name by your grand vizier.

Look in my eyes and see the tears well up
that are not feigned as my smiles have been. Your kind
and noble heart must move you to this action
as well as must your reasonable mind.
Mercy, I beg. It is brighter than any jewel
in the crowns that kings can wear who are rich but cruel.

The very air my people breathe in your land
shimmers in fear and pain. Their griefs destroy
the mind, the heart, and even the pious soul
that cannot praise what it does not enjoy.
As plants can take root in the cracks of a ruined wall,
tears from even the strongest faces fall.

You mean to be just in executing him
who subverted your laws. Let this same justice save
my people. Obey your gentle heart's impulse
and stop this business he still conducts from the grave.
There are thousands who cower in fear, powerless,
    nameless,
praying for pardon while knowing themselves to be
    blameless.

My people will be grateful to you, my lord,
respect your laws and hold you in high esteem,
offering freely what no regime can compel—
a part of that love they feel for the supreme
Lord of the universe who reigns on high
whose judgment we submit to when we die.

And think how the alternative is grim,
for when innocent men are punished, no one can feel
secure, and in desperation men conspire
in paranoid plots. Who then can tell the real
danger from an empty rumor? The air
turns acrid from the threats that are everywhere.

That was what Haman wanted, to give the wicked
strength to prey upon their betters, which
he trusted them to do—so he in turn,
extracting his share from each, could grow as rich
as any man in the kingdom, even you.
This mischief of his remains for you to undo.

Hear then the fervent prayer I address to you
and God in Heaven, that he may incline your mind
to mercy and justice. Spare my people's lives.
Let no innocent blood be shed in the blind
hatred man can show to his fellow man
as he has, I am sorry to say, since time began.

The goodness of the Lord preserves the skies,
the earth, and all its creatures, just as you,
as if you were one of the heavenly host of angels,
can in your wisdom and mercy also do . . . "
She can go no further. Passion and pity break
her heart and voice as she pleads for her people's sake.

Her words hang in the air and somehow refract
the silence of the great hall to beseige
the heart of the King's heart. Her delicate face
is not reproachful. He is her lord and leige,
but she, in her humility, is grand,
and all his powers are thus hers to command.

"Love," the King replies, "is a sun that dries
the noxious mists of night and the morning dew,
restoring the air to health. And from corruption's
fevers I am released, through love of you
and restored to health and sanity. The dank
miasma is gone, and I have you to thank.

The soft touch of your lips is restorative,
and the perfume of your hair, a powerful cure.
My spirit revives in me and I will live
a better happier life, virtuous, pure,
and flourishing in the warmth of your sweet gaze
that blesses my nights and glorifies my days.

What have I ever refused you? What desire
have you expressed that did not at once become
my own most fervent wish? What offering
have I not made from my imperium
on the altar of my love for you, the sole
article of my faith, and my soul's goal?

I can command my subjects, but you have the power
to order me, a king, to obey your whim.
You are the greater ruler: your light shines
so brightly that mine seems, beside it, dim."
He concludes his speech by putting into her hand
the golden scepter with which he rules the land.

The edict she wants repealed is revoked, undone—
and those who obey Haman's ukase will be
subject, themselves, to penalties most severe
that the Jews on their own may impose as they may see
right and fit to do. Thus Haman's curses
the King unsays, or better yet, reverses.

Her husband's answer is all that she could wish,
for Mordecai, her cousin, holds the seal
of state that Haman held, and his great wealth
devolves to him. Because of her appeal
the King has put an end to Israel's terror
as if he corrected some slight clerical error.

The clerks meanwhile are busy, setting down
the details of this newly promulgated
law. The seals are affixed, and riders sent
to the provinces where, it is anticipated,
there will be executions—but the King
has revised the list of names of those who will swing.

On the twenty-third day of the third month of the year,
this dispensation is published throughout the land
in all the various tongues of the many peoples
and read aloud so that all may understand
the Queen's proposal Mordecai has sealed
with the powers the King has given him to wield.

In every village- and town-hall, every barracks,
and every gendarmerie, on the bulletin board
the notice is posted that Jacob's house is no longer
beyond the laws' protection and that this is the word
of the King in council. And what man dares ignore
that king to whom he is sworn and is fighting for?

The Jews can scarcely believe this news. Their moans
of grief are stilled, and then comes the nervous laughter
miracles sometimes produce. To breathe again
in freedom is like a dream of the hereafter,
but this is not a dream; they are not sleeping;
and there is joy in their lives instead of weeping.

The messengers come again with the latest news
of what the King has ordered with heaven's assent—
it is decreed in Shushan that those who oppressed
or threatened Jews are liable to punishment.
The couriers' horses' hoofbeats pound as they ride
to publish the notice in town and countryside.

On the thirteenth day of the twelfth month, it is done—
this letting of blood in the rigorous satisfaction
of justice that the troubled soul has yearned for
and dreamed about. Now every heinous action
these wicked men had plotted is repaid
abundantly, as the King's law is obeyed.

One escapes from all but certain death, and the blood
flows back to the pallid cheek restoring the rose
of health and vigor. Meanwhile, on every side,
are scenes of carnage the grateful father shows
the terrified son in his arms, safe now from these
bad men and their depraved atrocities.

There is weeping—for joy, for the end of fear, for feelings
impossible to define or describe. The air
is sweet that they breathe, and the sun in the sky is bright.
They laugh, or are stricken dumb, or are moved to prayer,
to thank the Lord who has given them life again
or, after the blessing, only mumble, "Amen."

At the court, Mordecai standing beside the King
is splendid in white robes with purple trim.
A golden coronet is on his head,
and the populace rejoices seeing him
who has done well with the King and in his name
and deserves a share of the credit and the fame.

Each is a brilliant light, and the other seems
a reflecting mirror, or do they both shine bright?
Twin beacons in the darkness, are their gleams
separate phenomena to dazzle the sight
of the celebrating throng? Or is the one
the passive moon to the other's active sun?

The mood is one of thankfulness, as if
at harvest time in a prosperous bountiful year,
but the crop they gather up is Israel's children,
not only surviving but freed from their habit of fear.
There are tributes they offer the King and gifts that they
exchange among themselves on this great day.

At a wave of the King's hand, their faith is renewed,
and legal again in every province. The laws
forbidding their form of worship are all revoked.
Whose heart would not leap up for such a cause?
The terror is gone. And in through the same door
truth has returned to dwell forevermore.

Those who the day before were poor and afraid
are now empowered, can make a living, can walk
with their heads high, while those who jeered and scoffed
must beg for mercy, their faces white as chalk,
knowing what depth of evil they've done and how
little they merit the Jew's forgiveness now.

Collecting their forces, the Jews kill the ten sons of Haman
and more than five hundred in Shushan; the Queen asks that
another day be appointed for further executions in the man-
ner that Haman chose; the King assents, and seventy-five
thousand are put to death; Mordecai and the Queen proclaim
a day of fasting in commemoration of this miracle; and the
King prospers because of what he has done.

On the thirteenth day, it is fixed, of the year's twelfth
month, the arrow that evil has poisoned will go
to seek its mark. But its aim is different now,
and the victims are those who before wielded the bow.
Those who were weak are suddenly made strong
and bold as well, for they have suffered wrong.

The virtue in their hearts that was like a fragile
crystal is bright as ever, but hard as stone—
as diamond, say—and they rise up in their wrath
empowered at last by this edict from the throne.
Lambs given the lion's courage and pride
discover their honor that ought to be satisfied.

Think how a snake in the winter's cold is chilled
to torpor, all but lifeless, but then the rays
of the springtime sun will warm its blood. Its life
returns, and its strength and hunger, and it preys
on whatever warm-blooded creatures that have forgot
how fast a snake can be when the day is hot.

Thus are the sons of Zion returned to life
by the warmth of the King's regard. Their spirits rise
from the depths of their dejection, and they turn
their victimizers victims. For those cries
and groans of loved ones echoing still in their ears
they exact a louder antiphon of tears.

In all the provincial capitals, this campaign
is underway. The gentiles, terrified,
are snowmen in the sunshine, melting in
contrition's rivulets. Their icy pride
that liked to glare or sneer or condescend,
is humbled now and everybody's friend.

They fawn as they have always done, but now,
with Mordecai at the emperor's right hand,
they dance to a different tune. They carry out
the letter and the spirit of his command,
a rein on vice, a spur to the public good,
and a vision of universal brotherhood.

In Shushan itself, the pious Mordecai
who has ended the persecution considers the case
of those who were the persecutors, the wicked
enemies of justice and of his race.
What should be done with them whose towering guilt
looms like that courtyard gibbet Haman built?

The people arm and rove throughout the city
seeking those from whom they used to hide
to vent their righteous anger and repay them
with hurt for every hurt as is justified.
The gutters run with freshets of bright red.
In Shushan alone there are five hundred dead.

Among these are the sons of Haman: the poison
tree is felled but these ten are the shoots
and are cut down who might have carried on
the wicked schemes with which they were in cahoots.
The report comes to the King of the sorry end
of those who will never conspire again or offend.

He smiles and says to the Queen: "Into your pretty
ears I delight to deliver the happy news:
your people have avenged the evils done them.
Of those in Shushan who used to attack the Jews
five hundred who no doubt were guiltiest
are dead—and a good example to the rest.

My love is the gold setting; yours is the gem
that makes the ring so precious. What you ask
is a gift to me: you teach me how to please you;
my efforts are a pleasure, not a task.
Adoring you, I am fulfilled, am blessed
to be allowed to grant you your request.

As the flower's petals are to the bumblebee,
so are your lips to me: their nectar comes
of wise discourse to delight my ears and soothe
my troubled soul that, in its transport, hums.
Your words resound in silence, the perfume
of flowers that were lately in the room."

She answers, "Good my Lord, if it please you,
I am gratified by what you have done so far
in Shushan to carry out the law. But let
this be the model and the exemplar
of infamy's reward. Throughout the land
villainy still thrives at every hand."

Her will is what he wishes, or say her wish
is a law for him to ratify and proclaim.
The corpses of Haman's sons go on display,
and three hundred more in Shushan die in shame.
The Jews, being single-minded, execute
their enemies but they do not steal or loot.

Elsewhere, throughout the provinces, the sons
of Israel proceed with the work and slay
some seventy-thousand men, or even more.
Seventy-five thousand, some people say.
If enmity to Jews had been wide-spread,
those who were most hateful are now dead.

On the thirteenth of Adar are these things done,
but the fourteenth is a feast day, a celebration
of the end of fear and rebirth of hope and freedom.
It is as if a cloud that has covered the nation
is blown away and the rays of the sun break through
to a golden dawn for gentile as well as Jew.

Thus it is that in Shushan, the fifteenth day
is when the children of Jacob clean the blood
from their swords and rest, but in the countryside
the fourteenth is the day they receive the good
tidings and observe a day of leisure,
exchanging gifts, feasting, and taking pleasure.

Mordecai, devoted and zealous, watches
over the Jews in the capital and in remote
villages of the empire. He commands
the guards to be vigilant, while all the Jews denote
these days as sacred, that they might not forget
their deliverance from this most dire threat.

In the towns the people bow their heads in prayers
of thanks to Mordecai and the King but more
to the Being above, who in his infinite love,
has pitied them, sinful, undeserving, and poor,
showing them evil that lives in the hearts of men
along with goodness, too, and has saved them then.

A miracle? A sign of His love? Or is it
the case that love is a miracle always? We give
and receive gifts, to remind one another how Heaven
was moved to help us. The troubles through which we live
are governed by luck—which is not always blind: the
    depraved
are sometimes punished; the good sometimes are saved.

And the rationale is in those tablets Moses
received on Sinai that now are graven in
our hearts where their steady light shines in the darkness,
the clear instructions we need for avoiding sin
and living in such a way that we may earn
that heavenly approval for which we yearn.

The intercession of the Queen, the good
counsel of Mordecai, these were the means
by which the higher powers saved their people.
As the memory of evil lights the scenes
of happy life, more fervent is their prayer
of gratitude in Shushan and everywhere.

Proclaim it to the world, that the Lord's truth
is brighter than the sun and never sets.
The evidence of these miracles attests
the majesty of the Lord that a man forgets
going about his business from day to day,
unless he attends to what the old stories say.

On all his lands and his islands in the sea
the King imposes a special tax to remind
his subjects of his power they must obey,
the rich and proud, as well as the poor who may find
protection in the laws of the King who is,
as they deserve, the savior or nemesis.

Mordecai's honor the happy King proclaims
throughout the land to Medes and Persians as well,
second only to him who sits on the throne,
his friend, advisor, counselor and sentinel,
whose loyalty and wisdom ought to be
the model for all to follow scrupulously.

Ah, what a perfect example of that perfection,
what a powerful demonstration of your Power
and mercy that come to the rescue of those in extremis
in what they are certain must be their final hour!
The altar of your temple is far away
yet can we turn our faces toward it and pray,

in hope that our prayers will be heard and sorrows turned
to joy at having endured for your Name's sake
these trials. By our suffering we have borne witness to
your glory, reckoning every pain and ache
as another rung on Jacob's ladder. That goal
of Heaven brings comfort to every suffering soul.

Sometimes there can be deliverance. Our God
can rouse to anger—as Sennacherib once learned.
His host had encircled Zion and the Lord
killed them all. That Assyrian king returned
to Nineveh, where his children struck him down
as he worshipped his false god and they took his crown.

But mercy is what God loves, as David showed
when he spared the life of Saul at Engedi's cave
because the King was the Lord's anointed. See
how David was rewarded and be brave,
trusting in God, our shield, our fortified wall
who defends us from whatever blows may fall,

for surely he is opposed to wickedness,
and with his wings helps goodness soar as high
as our hopes should be in that ultimate salvation
established by his mercy. This is why
we adore him so. Wise, majestic, and strong,
may his Name be praised forever in our song.